A First Bible Story Book

Stories retold by
Mary Hoffman

Illustrated by
Julie Downing

This book belongs to

....

A Dorling Kindersley Book

*For Anna-Louise
and William*

DK

Dorling Kindersley
LONDON, NEW YORK, SYDNEY, DELHI,
PARIS, MUNICH and JOHANNESBURG

Project Editor Lee Simmons
US Editor Camela Decaire
Designer Sheilagh Noble
DTP Designer Almudena Díaz

Production Josie Alabaster
Managing Editor Jane Yorke
Managing Art Editor Chris Scollen

Religious Consultants Rev. Terence
Handley McMath, Donald Kraus,
Jenny Nemko

Additional design Jo Malivoire
Jacket design Linda Cole and Mark Haygarth

First American Edition, 1997
Paperback edition published in 2000
6 8 10 9 7

Published in the United States by
Dorling Kindersley Publishing, Inc.
375 Hudson Street
New York, New York 10014

Library of Congress Cataloging-in-Publication Data
Hoffman, Mary, 1945-
  A first Bible story book/retold by Mary Hoffman;
illustrated by Julie Downing – 1st American ed.
  p.cm – (Dorling Kindersley read and listen)
Originally published: New York: DK Pub., 1997.
  Summary: A collection of simple retellings of stories from
both the Old and New Testaments.
  ISBN 0-7894-5464-5 (pbk. + audio tape)
0-7894-6098-X (pbk. + CD)
  1. Bible stories, English. [1. Bible stories.]
I. Downing, Julie, ill. II. Title. III. Series.
BS551.2.H595 2000
220.9'505--dc21
                                      99-050388

Reproduced by Classic Scan
Printed and bound in China

For our complete
catalog visit
www.dk.com

Contents

Introduction to the Bible

The Bible is a collection of some of the best stories ever told. For hundreds of years they have been familiar to many readers. The stories are full of fascinating characters and exciting incidents and I have tried to tell them in ways that young children will find easy to understand. However, the Bible is different from other story collections. Not all of these retellings are happy, some are sad or even frightening. Therefore you may want to read each of the stories for yourself before reading them aloud. In this way you will be ready for any questions that might arise.

The Old Testament
The Old Testament stories are full of heroes like Noah, Abraham, Moses, and Daniel, who had a special relationship with God. Some, like Jonah, were reluctant heroes and had to be persuaded by strong means.

These stories are also full of vivid pictures – the glorious garden of Creation, the pairs of animals being marshaled into the ark, Joseph's coat of many colors. Some images are disturbing in their power, like Adam and Eve being banished from Eden, the near-sacrifice of Isaac by his father, and the lions who ate Daniel's accusers. But they are as much a part of the Bible as the more comforting imagery of creation, repentance, and salvation.

The New Testament

The imagery of the New Testament is familiar to most of us from Christmas cards and carols and from the Christian symbol of the cross. But the stories themselves are memorable, too.

An ordinary Jewish couple suddenly finds their lives turned upside down by an angel who explains that their child will be the son of God. As a baby, Jesus is visited

by important men with rich gifts and a powerful king wants to kill him. As a boy, he amazes people with his wisdom and learning. And as a man, Jesus is a great teacher and performs astonishing miracles, like feeding five thousand people with just five loaves of bread and two fish.

The New Testament moves from the promise of the first Christmas to its fulfillment in the pain and hope of the Crucifixion and Resurrection. The Easter story is not an easy one for young children, but we owe them the truth about what happened to the man who preached love, peace, and forgiveness. The sorrow of Jesus' death on Good Friday is followed quickly by the joy of his rising from the dead on the first Easter Sunday, and this is at the heart of Christian belief.

The Bible begins with Creation, and this Bible story collection ends with the Resurrection, both powerful images of fresh starts.

In writing **A First Bible Story Book** I have tried to convey some of the excitement and power of the well-known stories within a framework of hope and reconciliation.

Mary M. Hoffman

The Old

Testament

God Makes the World

In the very beginning, there was nothing but emptiness, darkness, and deep, deep water. Then God said the word, and the world was filled with light. He had made the first day.

But he saw that darkness was good, too, so he kept it and called it night.

On the second day, God divided up the water. Some he made the sea. The rest he put up in the sky. He made heaven to keep them apart.

On the third day, God put the seas in their proper places, and dry land between them. He told the earth to start growing trees and grass and plants.

On the fourth day, he made two big lights to hang in the sky – the sun by day . . .

and the moon by night. Then he made the stars that keep them company.

On the fifth day, God made all the creatures that live in the water – fish, whales, dolphins, and octopuses.

Then he made all the birds that fly in the air, from the great eagle to the tiny wren.

But the sixth day was the busiest of all. God made all the animals that live on the land. Not just the big ones, like buffaloes and elephants and tigers, but everything, right down to the smallest beetle

He decided to make some people, too, who would be like him. He made a man and a woman to take care of all the animals. God saw that the world he had made was good. On the seventh day, he rested.

that creeps through the grass.

The first man and woman were
Adam and Eve. God gave them a
wonderful garden called Eden. He told
them to eat fruit and plants and take care
of every single living thing in the world. He
told them that every person in the world
would come from them and their children.

The first job God gave Adam and Eve was to name all the animals. Imagine trying to choose the right name for the camel, the giraffe,

or the ostrich if you didn't know it already!

God visited Adam and Eve in the garden and talked to them. He gave them only one rule. "See that tree over there in the middle of the garden?" he asked. "It is the Tree of Knowledge. You must never eat its fruit. If you do, you will die."

Now there was a snake in the garden.
It slithered up to Eve and hissed,
"Why don't you pick that ripe
fruit from the tree in the
middle of the garden?"

Eve said, "God told us
not to. If we do, we will
die." "Nonsense," said
the snake. "This fruit
will help you know
things that God doesn't
want you to know."

14

The fruit looked tasty, so Eve picked one and took a big, juicy bite. It was so good she shared some with Adam. Right away, they felt shy and ashamed and realized they had no clothes on.

As soon as God realized they had eaten the forbidden fruit, a sadness as big as the whole world came over him.

He gave them clothes and sent them out of the garden to raise their children and live without ever seeing Eden again. To make sure they couldn't return, he set an angel with a fiery sword at the gate. And all because they had done the one thing he had asked them not to do.

Noah's Ark

Hundreds of years after Adam and Eve, the world had filled up with wicked people. This made God sad. He saw that there was only one good family left on the Earth: Noah, his wife, and their three sons, Shem, Ham, and Japheth.

God said to Noah, "I am going to send a great flood to wash the Earth clean. Everyone will be drowned except you and your family. You must build a big boat. You'll need space for a lot of food because there will be many animals to feed."

"Animals?" asked Noah. "Yes," said God. "Two of each kind, a male and female, including birds and creepy crawlies – even snakes."

God told Noah exactly how to build the boat, which was called an ark. Noah's whole family had to help – all his sons and their wives – because they would all be on the ark. They painted the wooden ark with sticky tar to keep the water out.

Noah's neighbors thought he was crazy. "A boat!" they laughed. "Haven't you noticed there's no sea around here?" But Noah kept on building.

As soon as the ark was ready, Noah took out his list of animals. His family had been rounding them up for weeks. How the neighbors stared! Two by two, the animals entered the ark.

The bears lumbered, the reindeer pranced, the giraffes swayed, and the snakes slithered.

The elephants were terribly slow, the lions padded along, the parrots squawked, and the wolves howled. The swift cheetahs passed right by the crawling crocodiles and leaping kangaroos

Soon the ark was alive with animals.
It was full of hay and oats and food for the
family, too. But the sky was getting very dark.
"Hurry up!" cried Noah to the waddling penguins.
As the tortoises crept up the gangplank, the first
drops of rain began to fall.

It was as if God had opened a window in heaven and poured water out. Rain cascaded from the sky, filling all the valleys. Thunder rumbled and lightning flashes cracked the sky in two.

For 40 days and 40 nights, rain drummed on the roof of the ark. Then one morning everything was quiet. The rain had stopped and the Sun was shining again.

The people who had laughed at Noah were now desperate to escape the rising water, but only the ark was lifted safely to the top of the swirling water, higher than the mountaintops.

The ark drifted for months. At last it bumped into some rocks. Slowly, the floodwaters sank down. Noah saw that the ark had settled on the high mountaintops of Ararat.

The animals couldn't wait to get off! But Noah wanted to be sure it was safe. Three times he sent a dove out from the ark.

The first time the dove flew straight back. The second time it had an olive leaf in its beak. The third time the dove didn't come back at all. It had found somewhere green and fresh to live. So Noah let down the gangplank and the animals bounded out of the ark.

As the birds flew away, Noah saw a beautiful arch of colors glowing in the sky. It was the first rainbow. God promised that he would never again destroy life on Earth – the rainbow would remind him of his promise.

Abraham and His Family

After the Flood, Noah's family grew and grew, peopling the Earth. One of these people became very special to God. The man's name was Abraham. His wife was Sarah.

One day, God sent for Abraham and told him that if he went where God led him, he would become the father of a great new nation.

Abraham was puzzled because he and Sarah had had no children, but he did as God told him.

Abraham gathered all his people together and, with Sarah and his nephew Lot, set out for Canaan. When they were nearly there, Lot and his people decided to turn to the East . . .

and Abraham and Sarah went to the West.

God spoke to Abraham again, telling him that all the land around him would belong to him and his family. He also said that Sarah would have a son. "Your family will be as many as there are stars in the sky," He said. Abraham was amazed. Surely Sarah was too old to have a child?

Sarah was very surprised to have a baby at last. They named their son Isaac.

When Isaac was still a little boy, God decided to give Abraham a terrible test. He wanted to see how much Abraham loved him. God told him to take Isaac up a high mountain and kill him. Abraham was horrified, and he could not tell Sarah what God had said.

He loaded a donkey and took Isaac with him as if they were just going out for a picnic.

Isaac carried wood, and they set off to climb the mountain.

When they had reached the top, Abraham built an altar and piled the wood on top. Isaac thought his father was going to kill a lamb. "Father, where is the lamb?" asked Isaac. "God will provide a lamb," said Abraham, but he could hardly speak for tears.

He set Isaac on the altar and took out his knife. The boy was terrified. Suddenly an angel called out, "Stop! Now God knows how much you love him – you were ready to give him your only son."
Looking up, Abraham saw a ram in the bushes, which he killed instead of Isaac.

Abraham had passed the test. He hugged Isaac tightly, then took him back home.

Joseph and His Rainbow Coat

When Isaac grew up he married Rebekah and they had twin sons, Esau and Jacob. Jacob, who was also called Israel, settled in Canaan and had a large family. His 12 sons were named . . .

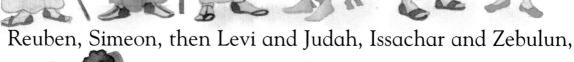

Reuben, Simeon, then Levi and Judah, Issachar and Zebulun,

Gad and Asher, Dan and Naphtali, then Joseph and Benjamin.

Joseph and Benjamin were Jacob's favorite children, but he loved Joseph best of all.

One day Joseph told his brothers about a dream he had had. They were tying up grain in the fields when . . .

. . . all the other brothers' bundles bowed down to Joseph's.

Joseph's dream made his brothers really angry. "Who does he think he is?" they grumbled.

Jacob had given Joseph a beautiful
coat, colored like a rainbow, and
that made the brothers even
more jealous. They hated
Joseph so much that some
of them wanted to
harm him.

So one day while they were working in
the fields, they grabbed Joseph and
tore his splendid coat off him.
They decided to kill
Joseph and throw
his body into a well.

But Reuben disagreed and said, "Let's just leave him at the bottom of the well." Reuben secretly meant to come back later and rescue Joseph.

Later, while Reuben was busy, the other brothers sold Joseph to some merchants who were traveling to Egypt.

Then the brothers smeared the rainbow coat with goat's blood and told Jacob his favorite son had been killed by a wild beast.

When the merchants reached Egypt, they sold Joseph to the captain of Pharaoh's guard. Joseph worked hard and after some years he was made head of the household.

One day, Pharaoh had a nightmare which no one could explain. God had shown Joseph what other people's strange dreams meant. So the Pharoah sent for him.

In Pharaoh's dream, seven fat cows came out of the river to graze.

Then seven thin cows followed the fat cows out of the water and gobbled them up. But the thin cows didn't get any fatter.

Joseph told Pharaoh that the dream meant Egypt was going to have seven years of good harvests followed by seven years of famine.

Pharaoh was so impressed by Joseph's explanation he put him in charge of building barns to store extra food for the bad years. And Pharaoh's dream came true, just as Joseph said.

33

Years later, during the famine, 11 visitors came from Canaan to ask for food. They were Joseph's brothers. He knew who they were immediately, but they had no idea who this powerful Egyptian was. Joseph decided to test his brothers to see if they had changed.

He gave them all the food they could carry, but in Benjamin's sack he hid a special silver cup.

The brothers set off for home, but they had not gone far when Joseph's guards rode after them and found the cup in Benjamin's sack.

The brothers were arrested and brought to Joseph. He pretended to be angry. "The rest of you can go free," he said, "but the one who stole my cup shall stay and be my slave."

The other brothers were horrified. Their father had already lost one of his favorite sons – it would break his heart if they went back without Benjamin. "Take one of us instead," they begged.

Then Joseph knew they had really changed. He told them who he was and asked them to fetch Jacob so they could all live together in Egypt.

Moses in the Bulrushes

Jacob's family, the Israelites, grew very large. Long after Joseph and his brothers were dead, there were lots of them living in Egypt. The new pharaoh did not like so many Israelites being in his country.

First he made them work as slaves. Then he ordered that all Israelite boy babies should be killed.

So Israelite women gave birth in secret. One family decided to save their newborn son in an unusual way. Even the baby's big sister, Miriam, was in on the plot.

They kept the baby hidden till he was three months old. By then he was sleeping less and it was hard to keep him a secret. So his mother wove a basket out of reeds. Miriam helped.

They coated the basket with mud and tar and let it dry. It was like a tiny boat.

The baby's mother put him in his little basket-boat and carried him to the river. She put the basket gently in the water, where it was half-hidden by bulrushes and reeds.

Pharaoh's daughter came down to the river to bathe, as she did at the same time every day. "What is that in the reeds?" she asked. "It looks like a basket."

One of her servants brought the basket to her. "It's a baby!" exclaimed the princess. "It must be one of the Israelite children. I shall save him and he shall be my son."

All this time, Miriam had been hiding in the reeds, watching out for her baby brother. "Your Highness," she said. "I know an Israelite woman who will nurse the baby for you."

"Good," said the princess. "The baby must have milk."

So the baby was taken care of by his own mother until he was old enough to go to the palace and live with Pharaoh's family.

The princess called the baby Moses, which means "taken from the water."

Daniel in the Lions' Den

The Israelites finally escaped from Egypt. But many years later they were again made slaves, this time by the Babylonian kings. One of the Israelites who still trusted God was Daniel.

Daniel was so honest and clever that the king, Darius, made him Prime Minister. All the other politicians were jealous.

They made Darius pass a law saying no one should pray to anyone but the king. Anyone who did would be thrown into a pit with hungry lions.

But Daniel went on praying to God the way he always had. Everyone could see him.

"Daniel prays to God," said the jealous politicians to Darius. "He has broken your law. You must throw him to the lions."

Darius was sad. He liked Daniel, but the law was the law.

He ordered Daniel to be thrown into the lions' den.

Next morning, the king went sadly to the lions' den, not daring to hope that Daniel had been saved.

"Daniel! Has your God kept you safe from the lions?"

42

"Here I am. God's angel stood between me and the lions."

The king ordered Daniel to be taken out of the pit. He had the politicians thrown in instead and the lions made short work of them, munching on their bones.

Then Darius ordered all his people to respect Daniel's God.

43

Jonah and the Big Fish

God watched over his Earth and saw that there were still bad things happening on it. He saw that the people of Nineveh were very wicked and violent.
He asked an Israelite teacher named Jonah to talk to them.

But Jonah didn't like that idea at all. He didn't want to go to Nineveh.

He ran away from God and boarded a ship that was going to Tarshish, in the other direction.

God knew that Jonah
was on the ship and
he sent a great
storm. All the
sailors were
terrified.

When Jonah realized
what was happening,
he told the sailors
that the storm was
his fault. "I tried to
disobey God," he said.
"You had better throw
me over the side."

The sailors didn't want to do
it, but Jonah made them throw him
into the water. Immediately the wind
dropped and the sea became calm.

Jonah fell through the waves, sure
that he was going to drown. All
of a sudden, a huge fish came
up and opened its jaws. Down . . .

and down and down

the dark . . .

through the water into

46

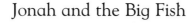

and around and around went Jonah, swirling and tumbling

until he ended up inside the fish's belly.

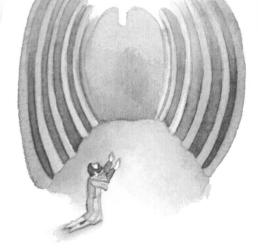

He fell on his knees and prayed to God, thanking him for saving him from the sea.

After three days and nights, God thought Jonah had learned his lesson. He made the fish swim to the shore . . .

and there it threw Jonah up onto the land. "Well?" asked God. "Now will you go to Nineveh?"

So Jonah walked all the way to Nineveh.

He warned all the people that God would destroy the city if they didn't stop doing bad things.

Everyone, even the king, was sorry. They all promised to lead better lives in the future. So God did not have to destroy the people after all. He was glad he could forgive them.

The New

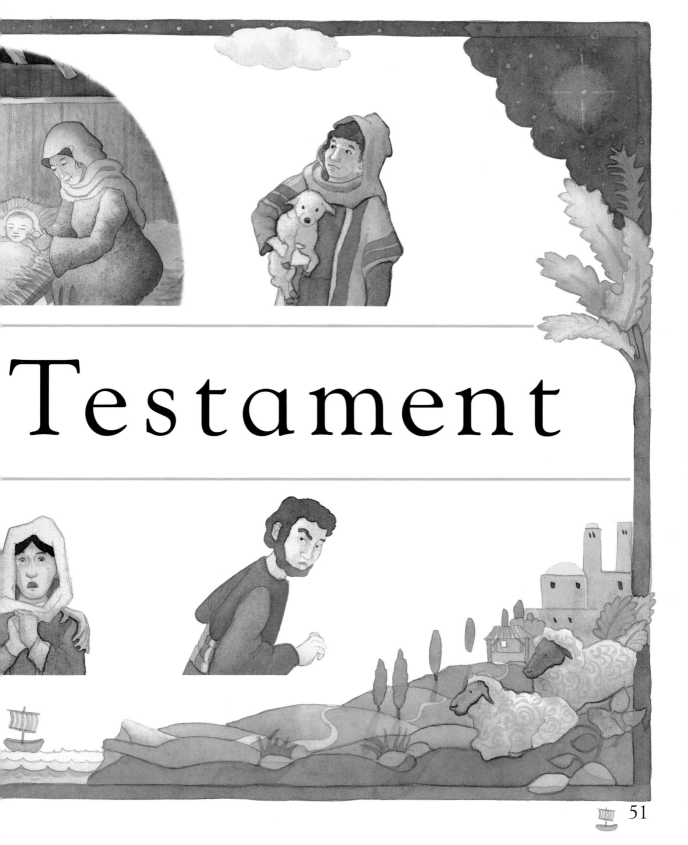

Testament

The First Christmas

When Herod was King of Judaea, there was a good, pure young woman living in the city of Nazareth, in Galilee. Her name was Mary and she was engaged to be married to a man named Joseph.

One day an angel came to Mary and told her she was going to have a baby. "But how?" asked Mary. "I am not married yet."

"This baby will be special. He will be the Son of God."

Mary did not understand, but she agreed to do what God wanted.

Joseph and Mary had to travel to Bethlehem. By then it was nearly time for Mary to have her baby.

They searched everywhere for a place to stay, but the city was crowded. Every inn was full.

But one innkeeper took pity on them when he saw that Mary was pregnant. "You can sleep in my stable," he said.

So the Son of God was born
in a stable, where cows
and donkeys were kept.

Mary wrapped the baby Jesus
in strips of cloth and put
him to bed in a manger
filled with fresh hay.

On the hills some shepherds were guarding their sheep. They were sitting together and dozing when suddenly the sky was filled with light and an angel appeared.

"Don't be afraid, there is great news! A baby has been born in a stable in Bethlehem. He will save all the world."

The shepherds were amazed. "A Savior?" they said. "In a stable?" They decided to go and see this wonderful sight for themselves.

So they took their flocks and
went down into Bethlehem . . .

straight to the stable where the
baby Jesus was. Later, they told
everyone the amazing things
they had seen and heard.

Mary never forgot that night
and thought about it often.

The Wise Men

When Jesus was born in Bethlehem, a new star appeared in the sky. The wise men in the East saw the star and knew a great king had been born.

The wise men followed the star all the way to Jerusalem.

They went straight to King Herod's palace and asked, "Where is the new king?" Herod was furious, but he pretended to be pleased.

"He isn't here," he said. "But do tell me when you find him."

Then the star led the wise men from Jerusalem to Bethlehem, where it stopped moving over the stable.

The wise men went inside and worshiped the baby Jesus. They gave him presents of gold, frankincense, and myrrh.

Later, God sent the wise men a dream that warned them not to see Herod again. So they traveled home a different way.

Joseph had a dream, too.
In his dream an angel
came to him.

"You are in danger! You must take Mary and Jesus and run away to Egypt."

So Joseph and Mary took
the baby Jesus and crept
out of the stable in the
middle of the night.

They set off for Egypt and no one
knew where they had gone.

Herod waited and waited, but the wise men did not return. He flew into a rage. He was king, not this baby.

He ordered his soldiers to kill all the baby boys in Bethlehem, just as Pharaoh had done with the Israelite babies in Egypt in the time of Moses. Jesus had escaped just in time.

But in the end, the wicked king died and it was safe for Mary and Joseph to bring Jesus back from Egypt.

Jesus Is Lost and Found

Jesus grew up happily in Nazareth. Joseph was a carpenter and made furniture in his workshop.

When he was bigger, Jesus helped Joseph in the workshop.

One day when Jesus was twelve years old, Mary and Joseph took him to Jerusalem for the Feast of the Passover.

When the feast was over, Mary and Joseph set off on the long journey back to Nazareth.

They had lots of friends and relations with them, so that almost a whole day passed before they realized that Jesus wasn't with them. He was lost!

Frantic with worry, Mary and Joseph turned back toward Jerusalem. They searched for Jesus for three whole days. At last, they went sadly to the temple . . .

. . . and there he was!

The boy was sitting with the oldest, wisest people, not just listening, but asking them questions. And they were asking Jesus questions, too, just as if he were a wise old man.

Mary and Joseph rushed forward.

"What have you been doing? We have been worried sick about you. We thought you were lost."

"You shouldn't have worried. I must do what my Father wants me to do."

Mary and Joseph did not really understand Jesus. Most of the time he was just an ordinary little boy. But Mary never forgot that he was special.

Five Thousand Hungry People

When Jesus grew up, he left his family and traveled all over the country telling people about God.

He chose some friends to join him. They were called his disciples.

One day, Jesus was preaching in a deserted place far from any town.

A huge crowd gathered to listen to him and more and more people arrived throughout the day.

By the evening there were about five thousand people there, and no one had anything left to eat.

"It is time to send the people away," said the disciples. "They must find food."

"Ask if anyone in the crowd has any food," said Jesus.

After a long search, the disciples found a little boy who had just arrived with his picnic. They brought him to Jesus. "This is all we can find," they told him.

Jesus blessed the food, then told the disciples to hand it out.

They looked into the basket and saw . . .

two small fish

and five barley loaves.

It didn't really look like enough food for five thousand people, but the disciples did as Jesus had asked.

It was astonishing. By the time everyone had eaten as much as they wanted, there were not one, not two, but . . .

one, two, three,

four, five, six,

seven, eight, nine,

ten, eleven, twelve baskets left over.

Imagine how the little boy felt! Everyone began talking about who Jesus could be to make such miracles happen.

69

The Last Supper

Jesus continued teaching people about God and it made some powerful people angry. They began to plot against Jesus to see if they could get rid of him.

One Passover, Jesus went to Jerusalem with his disciples.

When everyone was at the supper table, Jesus blessed the bread and the wine.

He gave them to the disciples, saying "This is my body and blood, which is given for you. Remember me."

Not everyone was pleased to see Jesus.

Some of the disciples went ahead and found a room where they could eat the special Passover meal together.

During the meal, Judas slipped away from the table quietly.

Jesus knew that Judas, one of the twelve disciples, was going to betray him to those people who hated him.

Jesus knew he was going to be killed, so he went to pray in a garden nearby. He asked his disciples to pray with him, but they fell asleep.

Later, Judas came and kissed Jesus. That was a sign for some soldiers, who came forward to arrest Jesus. When the disciples saw the soldiers, they ran away.

Jesus was taken to Pontius Pilate, the Governor of Judaea. "Are you the King of the Jews?" asked Pilate. "Yes, it is as you say," said Jesus.

Pilate said, "This man has done nothing wrong. He should not die." But the people shouted, "Crucify him!"

Pilate didn't want to be blamed for Jesus' death, but he chose to agree with the people's choice. Jesus was led away to his death.

The First Easter

The soldiers jammed a crown of thorns on Jesus' head and forced him to carry a wooden cross to a hill outside the city. They made a sign for the cross saying: THE KING OF THE JEWS.

Then Jesus was nailed to the cross. Two thieves were crucified beside him.

Jesus' mother, Mary, and his disciple John stood at the foot of the cross. Jesus asked John to look after Mary.

In great pain, Jesus asked God to forgive the people who had plotted to kill him. Then the sky turned black and the ground trembled. Jesus gave a loud cry and died.

One of the soldiers there, who saw all of this happen, said, "Truly, this man was the Son of God."

Jesus' friends gently took his body down from the cross and laid it in a cave. Then they rolled a huge stone across the mouth of the cave.

All the next day, which was Saturday, the Jews' holy day, Jesus' family and friends hid from the soldiers and cried because Jesus had died.

On Sunday morning they went to visit his tomb. But the stone had been rolled back and Jesus' body was gone.

Mary Magdalene, one of Jesus' closest friends, burst into tears at the thought that his body had been stolen. Then Mary saw a man that she thought was the gardener.

But he said to her, "Mary," and she recognized Jesus' voice. Jesus had risen from the dead!

The disciples saw Jesus, too, before he joined his Father in Heaven. They told many people about Jesus and God's love. Christians believe that Jesus was sent to die and rise again to save the world.

Who's Who in the Bible Stories

To help you find your way around **A First Bible Story Book**, here is a list of main characters and the pages where you'll find them. There's also a reference showing where the stories are in the Bible.

Old Testament

Adam and Eve   Page 12
Genesis 1-3
The first man and woman.

Noah   Page 16
Genesis 6-9
The only good man of his time. God decided to send a big flood to wash the world clean of wickedness. Only Noah, his family, and two of each animal were saved.

Shem, Ham, and Japheth   Page 16
Genesis 6-9
Noah's three sons.

Abraham   Page 24
Genesis 12-13, 17, 21-22
A descendant of Noah who had great faith in God. His son was called Isaac.

Sarah   Page 24
Genesis 12-13, 17, 21-22
Abraham's wife. God gave her a child when she was past child-bearing age.

Isaac   Page 26
Genesis 21-22
Son of Abraham and Sarah.

Lot   Page 25
Genesis 13
Abraham's nephew.

Rebekah   Page 28
Genesis 25
Isaac's wife. They had twin sons, Esau and Jacob.

Jacob   Page 28
Genesis 37, 42-45
The younger son of Isaac and Rebekah. He was married twice and had twelve sons. They were: Reuben, Simeon, Levi, Judah, Issachar, Zebulun, Gad, Asher, Dan, Naphtali, Joseph, and Benjamin.

Joseph and Benjamin   Page 28
Genesis 37, 39-45
Jacob's two youngest sons. Their mother was Rachel, the woman Jacob loved the most. Joseph always looked after his little brother Benjamin, even when they were grown up.

Pharaoh   Page 32, 36
Genesis 40-41, Exodus 1
The title given to the ruler of Egypt.

Israelites   Page 36
Exodus 1
Descendants of Jacob and his family.

Miriam   Page 36
Exodus 2
Moses' older sister.

Moses   Page 36
Exodus 2
An Israelite. Brought up as an Egyptian, he later became a leader of the Israelites.

Daniel   Page 40
Daniel 6
An important man in Babylon whose faith in God was put to the test.

Darius   Page 40
Daniel 6
A ruler in Babylon when Daniel was alive. He was a fair king, and was tricked into sending Daniel to the lions' den.

Jonah   Page 44
Jonah 1-4
An Israelite preacher and a reluctant hero. When God asked him to go to Nineveh, he refused. An adventure with a large fish changed his mind.

New Testament

Mary Page 52
Matthew 1-2, Luke 1-2
The mother of Jesus. She was a young girl in Nazareth when an angel told her that her baby would be the Son of God.

Joseph Page 52
Matthew 1-2, Luke 1-2
A carpenter from Nazareth who married Mary.

Jesus Christ Page 54
The New Testament
God loved the world so much that he sent his son, Jesus, to tell everyone about God and to save the world. The whole of the New Testament is about Jesus.

He taught people about the love of God and performed many miracles. Wicked men had him put to death, but he came back to life again. The Christian church was founded to spread his message.

The wise men Page 58
Matthew 2
Sometimes called the kings, or Magi. They were men from the East who studied the stars. A new star led them to baby Jesus.

Herod Page 58
Matthew 2
King of Judaea. He was a wicked man who had all the baby boys in Bethlehem killed when he heard a new king, Jesus, had been born.

Disciples Page 66
Matthew 14, 26; Mark 6, 14; Luke 9, 22; John 6, 13
Jesus had twelve followers, called his Disciples. They were Simon Peter, Andrew, James, John, Philip, Thomas, Bartholomew, Matthew, James, Thaddeus, Simon, and Judas Iscariot.

Judas Iscariot Page 71
Matthew 26, Mark 14, Luke 22, John 13, 18
A disciple; Jesus' betrayer.

John Page 74
John 19
The disciple who was closest to Jesus.

Pontius Pilate Page 73
Matthew 27, Mark 15, Luke 23, John 18-19
Roman governor of Judaea.

Mary Magdalene Page 77
Mark 16, John 20
A friend of Jesus. She was the first to see him when he rose from the dead.